Original title:
When Love Ends

Copyright © 2024 Swan Charm
All rights reserved.

Author: Kaido Väinamäe
ISBN HARDBACK: 978-9916-79-078-6
ISBN PAPERBACK: 978-9916-79-079-3
ISBN EBOOK: 978-9916-79-080-9

Unraveled Hearts

In shadows deep, we used to roam,
Now silence fills our once bright home.
Threads of laughter, now unwound,
Memories linger, lost yet found.

Once we danced beneath the moon,
Now echoes fade, we part too soon.
Cracks in the fabric, time reveals,
Unraveled hearts, our fate conceals.

The Weight of Goodbyes

A single tear, a heavy sigh,
Words unspoken, the reason why.
Promises made now slip away,
The weight of goodbyes, hard to say.

Moments cherished, fleeting days,
In the silence, memory stays.
Carried forward, the dreams we sow,
Yet deep inside, we still feel the glow.

Letters Left Unsent

In a drawer, old words remain,
Fragments of love, whispers of pain.
Ink stains the paper, thoughts untold,
Letters left unsent, dreams unfold.

Time has passed, yet feelings cling,
A silent heart, longing to sing.
What if the words had found their way?
Could they change our fate today?

Distant Stars

Across the night, they brightly gleam,
Wishes whispered, lost in a dream.
Distant stars twinkle high above,
Guiding lost souls back to love.

Every glance brings stories near,
A cosmic dance, a cosmic sphere.
We reach for dreams that seem so far,
Yet find our way, like those bright stars.

The Last Page Turned

In silence, I turn the last page,
Whispers of stories fade away.
Memories dance in twilight's glow,
A chapter closes, night meets day.

With ink that bleeds in faded dreams,
Lines of laughter, tears entwined.
Each word a heartbeat, softly screams,
In the depths of a weary mind.

The fragrance of paper, time's embrace,
Echoes linger in shadowed halls.
Lost in the echoes, a familiar place,
Where joy and sorrow softly calls.

Every ending births a new start,
Pages written in the heart's own hand.
In the quiet, I feel the art,
Of the stories left upon the sand.

So here's to the tales that slip away,
In the dust of the shelf, they shall rest.
For every last page leaves a ray,
Of hope that lingers in each quest.

Remembering What Was

In echoes of time, I find my way,
Through whispers of laughter, shadows dance.
A flicker of moments, sun-kissed day,
Reminds me of youth and a fleeting chance.

The taste of summer, sweet and light,
Laughter like ripples on a calm lake.
Captured in frames, a cherished sight,
Every heartbeat, a decision to make.

Memories twirl in a gentle breeze,
Soft as the petals that fall from the trees.
Each face, each place, a tender tease,
Awakening warmth that never flees.

I wander the paths of once upon dreams,
Searching for echoes of what still gleams.
Through windows of time, the sunlight beams,
Illuminating the fabric of schemes.

Yet time, the thief, takes treasures away,
In the heart, they will endlessly stay.
For remembering what was, come what may,
Is the canvas of life in shades of gray.

The Echo of Silence

In the stillness of the night,
Whispers drift without a sound.
Shadows dance beneath the light,
Life's quiet pulse can be found.

Every heartbeat echoes clear,
In the void, a secret sings.
Silence wraps its warmth so near,
Cradling hopes on whispered wings.

Moments fade, yet linger on,
In the gaps, our dreams reside.
Echoes rise with every dawn,
In the hush, we softly hide.

Through the quiet, truths are born,
Silhouettes that softly blend.
In the silence, hearts are worn,
Finding peace that will not end.

Shattered Reflections

Mirrors cracked, the truth revealed,
Fragments of a time long lost.
In each shard, the heart concealed,
Every glance reflects the cost.

Faces blurred, a past unkind,
Echoes of what used to be.
In the pieces, love defined,
Shattered hopes drift aimlessly.

Time unveils a scarred façade,
Promises once bright now fade.
In the dark, the light seems flawed,
Shadows cloak the plans we made.

Through the chaos, visions weave,
Stories told in silent screams.
In the night, we still believe,
Picking up our broken dreams.

Faded Whispers of Two

Underneath the starry sky,
Voices soft, a secret shared.
Fingers touch as moments fly,
In this space, we both are dared.

Time slips by like grains of sand,
Memories woven, sweet and thin.
In the quiet, we both stand,
Lost in where the dreams have been.

Each word spoken, gentle sighs,
Holding on to what is true.
In the dusk, our laughter lies,
Faded whispers of me and you.

Though the world may shift and change,
Hearts will hold what's tried and tested.
In these echoes, we remain,
Paths entwined, forever rested.

The Last Embrace

In the twilight's softest glow,
Two shadows linger, side by side.
Knowing well the tales of woe,
Hearts full of secrets, love and pride.

Time has carved its tale in stone,
Yet in this moment, we can breathe.
In the silence, we're not alone,
Holding close what we believe.

With each heartbeat, warmth ignites,
An unspoken promise unfolds.
In this dance beneath the lights,
The last embrace, forever holds.

As the stars begin to weep,
We find strength in what's about,
In the depths, our spirits leap,
Love remains, we have no doubt.

The Pause After the Storm

The sky exhaled a tender sigh,
As clouds drifted slowly away.
Sunlight painted the world anew,
In the silence, hope found its way.

Puddles held reflections bright,
Nature whispered soft and low.
A promise borne on the breeze,
In stillness, the heart starts to grow.

Birds returned with joyful song,
Branches swayed in gentle dance.
Life awoke from restless dreams,
In this moment, we took a chance.

The air was fresh, a sweet embrace,
Each heartbeat syncs with the dawn.
We learned to cherish every breath,
In the calm, we moved on and shone.

For storms may come and storms may go,
Yet strength is found in the reprieve.
Embrace the peace that follows pain,
In the stillness, we believe.

Tides of Memory

Waves washed ashore with stories untold,
Whispers of love, echoes of years.
Each grain of sand holds the dreams,
Married with laughter and tears.

The moonlight dances on restless seas,
Calling to hearts adrift at night.
In the rhythm of the ocean's pulse,
We find solace in the light.

Footprints fade but never depart,
The tides remember what we leave.
Each rise and fall tells a tale,
Of moments that taught us to believe.

With every crest, a memory flows,
Searching for shores we once knew.
In the depths of our quiet thoughts,
The tides still carry me and you.

As long as the ocean breathes and sighs,
We'll navigate these waters wide.
With love as our compass and guide,
Forever cherished, deeply tied.

Lingering Footsteps

Through silent halls where shadows fall,
Footsteps echo soft and slow.
Each room a chapter, each door a tale,
In the spaces where memories grow.

Dust dances in the muted light,
A fleeting glimpse of days gone by.
Whispers of laughter, a gentle breeze,
In the stillness, the heart can sigh.

A faded picture, a fraying edge,
Time has brushed its gentle hand.
Yet love remains, an everlasting thread,
Binding us in this sacred land.

Among the remnants of the past,
We find our strength, our grounded place.
In the lingering footsteps we leave,
Echoes of love we can't erase.

So let us wander through these halls,
With hearts wide open to explore.
For every journey leads us home,
In the footsteps that we adore.

Lost in the Rearview

The road stretches long beneath the sun,
Mirages dance on asphalt dreams.
With each mile, the past slips away,
Guided by hope and the quiet streams.

Reflections flicker in the glass,
Ghosts of moments that came and went.
Yet each turn shows the way ahead,
Lessons learned, and time well spent.

In the distance, shadows linger,
But forward is the path we choose.
Life is a journey, not a race,
Embrace the roads, the twists, the blues.

With every sunset, the day redeems,
A promise of tomorrow's light.
We look back fondly, yet venture forth,
Finding joy in the fading night.

So let the rearview mirror fade,
As we chase horizons rich and grand.
In living fully, we find our peace,
Lost no longer, together we stand.

The Last Dandelion Seed

In the breeze it takes flight,
A whisper of the sunset's light.
Carried far on gentle air,
To find a home, to land somewhere.

Once among the golden blooms,
Now a dream in twilight's glooms.
Hopes of spring through winter's chill,
To rise again, to bend the will.

Scattered dreams on fields unknown,
Where wildflowers have overgrown.
The last seed dancing through the skies,
With every breath, it softly flies.

It knows the song of distant lands,
As nature weaves with its own hands.
A story told without a sound,
Of life and love, forever bound.

Remnants of a Shared Sky

Beneath the same vast dome we gaze,
In twilight's touch, love gently stays.
Colors blend in soft embrace,
In the silence, we find our place.

Stars whisper secrets from above,
Echoes of laughter, whispers of love.
Time may change the paths we tread,
But memories linger, softly spread.

The clouds, they drift, like dreams we chase,
In every shadow, in every space.
Together bound by threads unseen,
In the heart's realm, where we have been.

Fragments of laughter float like dust,
In the realm of hope and trust.
No distance can sever the ties we've spun,
In the skies shared, we are never undone.

Familiar Strangers

In crowded rooms, we pass like ghosts,
Eyes meet briefly; we play no hosts.
Once we were brighter, now we are dim,
In an unspoken realm, we quietly swim.

Strangers in memories, shadows in light,
What was our story, wrong or right?
Familiar faces in places afar,
Once walked together, now just a scar.

Time has woven its intricate art,
Keeping us captive, pulling apart.
A nod, a smile, a fleeting glance,
Remnants of a forgotten dance.

In the silence, we share a sigh,
Two intertwined souls asking why.
Though paths diverge, and roads may bend,
In the heart's whisper, we can mend.

The Fading Rose

Once stood proud in a garden fair,
With petals soft, beyond compare.
But time, a thief in shadows cast,
Leaves behind what cannot last.

Fingers trace the faded hue,
Memories wrapped in morning dew.
A fragrance lost, a tale untold,
In every layer, the truth unfolds.

Beauty fades like twilight's glow,
In every season, we come to know.
Yet in each wrinkle lies a story,
Of fleeting moments, of past glory.

A promise held within decay,
New life waiting to find the way.
The petals fall, but roots remain,
In the heart's garden, love is not in vain.

Fading Embers

In the hearth of night,
Glows the past, dim light.
Memories softly fade,
Like whispers in the shade.

Stars blink in the dark,
Each a fading spark.
Ashes tell a tale,
Of love that starts to pale.

Time drifts like a breeze,
Carrying with such ease,
Embers lose their heat,
With shadows as their fleet.

Yet in the quiet glare,
A flicker still lays bare.
Hope dances on the edge,
Of a forgotten pledge.

Though flames may dwindle low,
In hearts, a steady glow.
Love's warmth remains inside,
In the dark, we abride.

The Last Whisper

A breath upon the air,
So soft, filled with care.
Words left unspoken,
Promises now broken.

Shadows stretch and sway,
In twilight's gentle play.
Silence grips the night,
While stars blink in their flight.

Echoes of the past,
In the stillness cast.
Hearts beat slow and true,
Bearing the weight of two.

But in that final breath,
A hint of life, not death.
Hope lingers in the gloom,
A flower in full bloom.

In every tender sigh,
Love's light will never die.
Though whispers may grow dim,
Their song forever brim.

Ghosts of Us

In corridors of time,
We wander, lost in rhyme.
Echoes of laughter blend,
With shadows that won't end.

Memories lie in wait,
For chance to re-create.
Familiar specters roam,
In the heart, our home.

Footsteps softly tread,
Where once our dreams were wed.
Through the veil of the night,
Our spirits take their flight.

Yet among the remains,
The joy still entertains.
Ghosts of us endure,
In love, forever pure.

A dance across the years,
Through laughter and through tears.
Though time may take its toll,
You'll always be my soul.

A Symphony of Silence

In a world so loud,
We find peace, unbowed.
Quiet whispers rise,
Beneath the endless skies.

Notes of stillness play,
As day turns into grey.
Harmony in dusk,
In the silence, we trust.

Stars twinkle, unseen,
In the fabric of dream.
Each heartbeat's a song,
In the silence, we belong.

With every breath we take,
A symphony we make.
In the void, we find strength,
In silence, we go length.

Though the night may fall,
In our hearts, we hear the call.
The beauty lies within,
In silence, we begin.

Behind Closed Doors

Secrets whispered soft and low,
In hidden rooms where few may go.
Love and pain entwined in sighs,
Behind closed doors, the truth often lies.

Faces mask their silent cries,
While laughter hides unspoken ties.
Moments shared, yet alone they'll stay,
Behind closed doors, dreams drift away.

Shadows dance, a fleeting glance,
Life's fragile threads, a quiet chance.
In the stillness, hearts will soar,
Behind closed doors, we search for more.

Trust woven deep, the heart confides,
In this world where silence abides.
Hopes and fears in tandem soar,
Behind closed doors, life's endless chore.

Conversations fade with the light,
And in the dark, we face the night.
With every unlock, a heart restores,
Behind closed doors, love's timeless shores.

The Quiet After the Storm

The world breathes deep, the air is still,
Nature's wrath has bent to will.
Raindrops linger on the ground,
In silence, peace is softly found.

Leaves once torn now dance anew,
Colors brightened by morning dew.
In the calm, the heart will mend,
The quiet holds what storms do send.

Echoes fade of thunder's roar,
Birds return to sing once more.
In every shadow, light will play,
The quiet brings a brand new day.

Reflections left in puddles spin,
Whispers of where we've been.
Sorrow sheds its heavy crown,
The quiet after lifts us up, not down.

Hope emerges, a tender seed,
In every heart, a longing need.
From chaos, beauty grows and swells,
The quiet after the storm compels.

A Tapestry of Wistfulness

Threads of memory softly weave,
A tapestry of dreams we leave.
Colors fading, stories told,
In wistfulness, our hearts unfold.

Moments linger, shadows cast,
Caught between the future and past.
Time's gentle hand, a weaving art,
A tapestry that tugs the heart.

Each stitch holds a whispered sigh,
A song of days gone meekly by.
Patterns change, but love remains,
In wistfulness, we break the chains.

Every thread a tale to tell,
In laughter and in sorrow's swell.
Brightest hues and darkest tones,
A tapestry composed of bones.

In every corner, hope revived,
In wistfulness, we feel alive.
A fabric rich with every tear,
A tapestry that draws us near.

Shadows in the Light

As sunlight spills through leafy arms,
Shadows play their subtle charms.
In the glow, dark forms will dance,
Shadows in the light take their chance.

Whispers echo in the beams,
Where hope and worry blend in dreams.
Silhouettes of what could be,
Shadows in the light, wild and free.

Moments flicker, time stands still,
In between the light, a chill.
Yet in their depths, we find our sight,
Shadows in the light spark delight.

Every shimmer holds a tale,
In the glow, fears often pale.
Intertwined in day's embrace,
Shadows in the light find their place.

A delicate dance of day and night,
Where darkness cedes to morning's fight.
In every heart, there's a spark so bright,
Shadows in the light—what a sight.

Wishes and Wounds

In the quiet of heart's despair,
Wishes whisper, weighing air.
Dreams unspoken, lost in time,
In shadows deep, they softly chime.

Wounds awaken in daylight's glow,
Haunting echoes of what we know.
Faded hopes like autumn leaves,
Rustle softly, as the heart grieves.

Yet in the dark, a flicker gleams,
Faint reminders of our dreams.
Wishes linger, a fragile thread,
Binding the wounded, even when bled.

Each scar tells stories, of paths we chose,
With every sorrow, a flower grows.
In the tapestry of pain and grace,
Wishes and wounds, a sacred space.

In the Wake of Us

In the stillness, memories call,
Echoes whisper, rise and fall.
Moments linger, heavy with weight,
In the wake of us, we hesitate.

Footsteps fade on cobblestone,
Silent shadows, all alone.
Conversations left unspoken,
In the wake, our hearts are broken.

Time weaves a tale of love untold,
In New Year's light, it turns to gold.
Hands once clasped, now drift apart,
In the wake of us, a fractured heart.

Yet in the dark, a flicker remains,
Memories weave through joy and pains.
In the laughter, in the cries,
In the wake, our spirit flies.

Patterns of Absence

In empty rooms where silence dwells,
Patterns emerge, like whispered spells.
Footprints linger, yet they fade,
In the shadows, memories played.

Fragments scattered, hearts unfold,
Tales of warmth, now icy cold.
Veils of absence drape the light,
In the silence, longing bites.

Each corner holds a ghostly trace,
Moments lost, no warm embrace.
The echoes form a haunting dance,
In patterns subtle, we take a chance.

Yet from the void, a voice might rise,
Finding strength beneath the skies.
In absence, hope will pierce the night,
Patterns of love, a guiding light.

The Language of Cold Nights

In the hush of winter's breath,
Words escape, a dance with death.
Stars above, like frozen tears,
Speak the language of our fears.

Each chill that bites, a poignant tale,
Of hearts entwined, but now grown frail.
Fires flicker, warmth held tight,
In the language of cold nights.

Letters written in frost and snow,
Softly whispering love's threshold.
Promises made beneath the moon,
Find their voice in a lonely tune.

Yet in the dark, where shadows play,
Hope ignites with the break of day.
The language shifts, as seasons turn,
In cold nights, the warmest yearn.

Unraveled Threads

In a tapestry of dreams, we weave,
Colors bright, some we believe.
Yet, gentle hands begin to fray,
Silent whispers fade away.

Fragile knots of memories bind,
Moments linger, slowly unwind.
Every stitch tells a story grand,
Yet slips through like grains of sand.

Fleeting glances in the night,
Promises lost to fading light.
Through tangled paths, hearts may stray,
As the threads come undone, decay.

In the silence, echoes roam,
Searching for a place called home.
But with every step, shadows creep,
In the unraveling, secrets keep.

The fabric of us, now laid bare,
What was once whole, hangs in the air.
A final touch upon the seam,
In the stillness, we dare to dream.

Conversations in Shadows

In the corners where silence dwells,
Voices linger, casting spells.
Whispers tangled, soft and low,
In the dark, their secrets flow.

Eyes that meet, a fleeting glance,
In the shadows, thoughts advance.
Words unspoken hang in air,
A silent promise, a hidden stare.

Beneath the stars, the night unfolds,
Each moment caught, a story holds.
Glimmers of truth in half-lit rooms,
In the quiet, a spark blooms.

Hearts converse where no one sees,
In the rustle of the trees.
A language weaves through night's embrace,
In its depths, we find our place.

When dawn arrives, these shadows fade,
But the echoes of us will not degrade.
In every pause, our souls appear,
In conversations only we hear.

The Weight of Unsaid Goodbyes

In the stillness where moments pause,
Lingers a weight without applause.
Words that tremble, stuck inside,
Goodbyes linger, hearts collide.

Paths taken turn into dust,
In the silence, we place our trust.
Heavy hearts with tales undone,
In every parting, battles won.

Memories cling like morning dew,
As we question what is true.
Unraveled futures, dreams deferred,
In every heartbeat, the unsaid heard.

Promises made on fleeting breath,
Tethered to life and woven depth.
Yet in every sigh, shadows creep,
In the weight of goodbyes, we weep.

As the final curtain draws near,
We stand trembling, stilled by fear.
But in that pause, love will abide,
In the weight of unsaid goodbyes.

A Portrait of Parting

In the frame of a dream's embrace,
Brushstrokes of time, a fleeting grace.
Each hue whispers tales we know,
Of laughter shared in the afterglow.

Faded colors blend and part,
A canvas painted from the heart.
In solemn hues, the sorrow's trace,
A portrait of moments we can't replace.

The brush that dances in despair,
Strokes of love that linger in air.
As the edges blur, memories fade,
In this picture, our truth is laid.

Beneath the surface, emotions swell,
In this silence, a story to tell.
Where paths diverge, our souls entwined,
A masterpiece of love, refined.

Though the frame may catch the light,
Within its borders, shadows ignite.
A portrait drawn with every sigh,
In the beauty of parting, we learn to fly.

The Journey Backwards

In shadows deep, we find our way,
Echoes whisper of yesterday.
Paths once traveled, now grown dim,
Memory's light, a fragile hymn.

Each step retraced, a tale unfolds,
Forgotten dreams, like stories told.
Winding roads of past and pain,
In silence, laughter, loss, and gain.

Familiar faces, lost in time,
Resonate softly, like ancient chime.
With every glance, a heart does ache,
As the past beckons, we start to break.

Yet in this maze, we learn, we grow,
Lessons learned from long ago.
Through tears and smiles, we reclaim,
The journey backwards, never the same.

So hold my hand, let's wander slow,
Through memories rich, in twilight's glow.
With every heartbeat, we'll explore,
The journey backwards, forevermore.

Dusty Photo Albums

On shelves they wait, in quiet stacks,
Dusty photo albums, memories cracked.
Faded smiles on yellowed pages,
Timeless moments from distant stages.

A child's laughter, a lover's gaze,
Captured time in a golden haze.
Each picture tells a silent tale,
Of love and loss, of hearts that sail.

Flip the page, and memories surge,
Past and present softly merge.
Faces lost, yet spirits shine,
In every corner their stories intertwine.

Yet as we browse through life's design,
We tread the lines of yours and mine.
Each snapshot holds a place, a spark,
In dusty albums, love leaves its mark.

So let's hold these treasures tight,
Through fading colors, they ignite.
For in the dust, we find our way,
In photo albums, yesterday stays.

The Other Side of Forever

Beneath the stars, we dare to dream,
Of moments lost, where shadows gleam.
A whisper carried on the breeze,
The other side holds mysteries.

We chase the dawn with hopeful hearts,
In every ending, a place it starts.
Time stretches out like fragile thread,
Connecting dreams to words unsaid.

Yet on this path, we may stumble,
While the universe begins to tumble.
Through darkness deep, we seek the light,
The other side of endless night.

With every step, a choice we make,
In every breath, it's ours to take.
Forever lingers, both near and far,
Guiding us like a wishing star.

So hold on tight, let love lead on,
Through twists and turns till fears are gone.
For on this journey, together we'll soar,
To the other side of forever, evermore.

Faded Love Letters

In drawers tucked, they softly lie,
Faded love letters, dreams awry.
Ink has blurred, but feelings stay,
Whispers of love from yesterday.

With trembling hands, we read the words,
Each syllable like singing birds.
Promises made in secret night,
Now echoes lost in fading light.

Once they sparked a flame so bright,
Now shadows dance, a silent fight.
Yet in the lines, our hearts ignite,
Faded love letters, still hold tight.

Through time and distance, we remain,
Hearts entwined, through joy and pain.
In every fold, a story shared,
Love letters faded, but never spared.

So take a moment, breathe it in,
These precious words hold where we've been.
For in their silence, love can mend,
Faded letters that never end.

An Unraveling Spell

Whispers dance upon the breeze,
Secrets wrapped in twilight's ease.
Fingers trace the stars above,
Casting charms of fleeting love.

Shadows weave a tale untold,
Binding hearts in threads of gold.
With every breath, the spell unfolds,
A mystery in silence holds.

Moonlit paths of dreams collide,
In the dark, there's nowhere to hide.
Each heartbeat a reverberating ring,
Echoing the promises we bring.

Time slips through like grains of sand,
Leaving traces on which we stand.
But in the night, our spirits soar,
In magic's grip forevermore.

Yet as dawn breaks, shadows shrink,
We realize what we can't think.
The spell unravels, dreams take flight,
Lost in the chaos of morning light.

The Footprints Left Behind

Footprints etched upon the shore,
Stories whispered, forevermore.
Each step a memory, each grain a dream,
Fleeting moments, like a silent scream.

The tide comes in, it sweeps away,
Yet echoes linger, never stray.
In the sand, a tale remains,
Of laughter, joy, and whispering pains.

With every wave that crashes down,
The footprints fade, yet love's renown
Leaves shadows cast in fleeting light,
A dance of day turning into night.

Reminders of where we have been,
Marks of laughter, traces of sin.
Each step forward, a bittersweet bind,
In the journey, what do we find?

So let us walk on paths anew,
With every sunrise lighting the view.
Though footprints fade, memories spark,
In our hearts, we forever embark.

A Canvas of Broken Promises

Brush strokes wild on a canvas bare,
Colors clash with an aching flare.
Every promise, a shattered hue,
Fragments of dreams once bright and true.

A palette drips with tales untold,
In the silence, the heart turns cold.
Each stroke a whisper of what's been lost,
A price we paid, a heavy cost.

Splattered hopes, a tangled weave,
In the chaos, it's hard to believe.
Yet through the cracks, new light can bloom,
A chance to rise from the silent gloom.

So paint anew with colors bold,
Craft a narrative yet to unfold.
In every shard, there lies a spark,
A chance to leave behind the dark.

With every layer, healing starts,
A masterpiece forged from broken parts.
On this canvas, life finds a way,
To shine through shadows, come what may.

Echoes of Your Laughter

In the quiet of the night,
I hear your laughter's grace,
A melody so bright,
It lingers in this space.

Shadows dance upon the wall,
Whispers soft and low,
Your joy, it fills the hall,
A tune I long to know.

Memories like fireflies,
Twinkling in the dark,
Your smile lights up the skies,
Each moment leaves a mark.

Through the echoes of the past,
I cherish every sound,
Your laughter holds me fast,
In dreams, you are unbound.

Though time may drift away,
And silence may descend,
Your laughter's sweet bouquet,
In my heart, will never end.

Autumn Leaves Falling

Golden hues adorn the trees,
As whispers fill the air,
Each leaf dances in the breeze,
A moment, fleeting, rare.

Crispness lingers on the ground,
A quilt of rust and gold,
Nature's beauty all around,
A story to be told.

Under skies of muted gray,
The world begins to slow,
With each leaf that drifts away,
A memory bestowed.

Time weaves gently through the air,
As days cut short the light,
In the chill, we find a care,
That wraps around us tight.

Autumn whispers soft goodbyes,
As winter starts to call,
With every leaf that falls and sighs,
We witness nature's all.

A Canvas of Regret

Brushstrokes faded on the page,
Each color tells a tale,
Of choices made, a silent sage,
In shadows I unveil.

The palette holds a bittersweet,
A mix of joy and pain,
Where dreams and fears together meet,
In whispers of the rain.

Strokes that linger in the night,
Haunting as they fade,
A canvas torn between the light,
And all that I evade.

Yet within this work of heart,
Lies beauty in the flaw,
For every end can be a start,
In every line, a law.

With each new dawn, I strive to paint,
With colors bold and true,
To find the grace in scenes that haunt,
And start my life anew.

The Space Between Us

In the silence, I can feel,
The distance stretching wide,
An echo of what was so real,
Where love and hearts collide.

Time ticks softly, ever slow,
In moments unforeseen,
Two souls adrift, with nowhere to go,
Caught in this in-between.

Memories wrap like tender threads,
Binding us, yet apart,
In whispered words that go unsaid,
I hide within my heart.

Stars above bear witness still,
To dreams we left behind,
Yet in this vast and aching chill,
A light begins to grind.

Though space may stretch, love bends anew,
In every beat, it grows,
And in this silence, I find you,
A bond the distance knows.

The Heart's Aftermath

In silence, echoes softly weep,
A heavy heart, secrets to keep.
Memories linger, shadows fall,
The aftermath of love's cruel call.

Broken dreams in pieces lie,
Promises lost beneath the sky.
Wounds that time cannot erase,
Leave a haunting, empty space.

Once bright flames now embers cold,
Stories filled with love retold.
In the stillness of the night,
Broken hearts still seek the light.

A gentle touch, a fleeting glance,
In every move, a broken dance.
Yet hope remains, a flicker bright,
Guiding souls through endless night.

As dawn breaks, the heart must mend,
Finding strength to love again.
Through every tear, a stronger thread,
In the heart's aftermath, we're led.

Lingering Shadows

Underneath the fading light,
Whispers linger, soft yet tight.
In the corners where dreams reside,
Shadows dance, they will not hide.

Echoes of laughter in the air,
Moments passed, yet linger there.
Time moves on, but memories cling,
In every note, the heart will sing.

Footsteps fading down the lane,
Leaving traces of joy and pain.
Lingering shadows, never gone,
Breathe life into the distant dawn.

In every gaze, a story told,
A tapestry of brave and bold.
Through the dusk, the past remains,
Lingering shadows, love's refrains.

As daylight breaks, they still persist,
In every heart, a tender twist.
With every dusk, they softly play,
Lingering shadows guide the way.

The Twilight Soliloquy

In twilight's grasp, we softly sigh,
As day gives way to starry sky.
Thoughts collide, a whispered plea,
In this moment, just you and me.

The world grows dim, our voices low,
Sharing dreams in gentle flow.
Nature hums a soothing tune,
As shadows dance beneath the moon.

Secrets spill like grains of sand,
In this twilight, hand in hand.
Each word spoken, a fragile thread,
In the soliloquy, we're led.

A breath of night, so rich, so sweet,
Echoes of love, a rhythmic beat.
With every heartbeat, silence speaks,
In twilight's glow, the soul still seeks.

As stars emerge, our hearts unfold,
Timeless tales of love retold.
In the dusk, where dreams align,
The twilight soliloquy is divine.

Words Unspoken

In quiet rooms where shadows play,
Words unspoken find their way.
In the silence, truths reside,
Hearts in longing cannot hide.

A gentle glance, a fleeting breath,
Hints of love that linger yet.
Unsaid moments, pure and rare,
Hang in the stillness of the air.

Each heartbeat feels the weight untold,
In every silence, stories unfold.
To whisper softly or to shout,
The words remain, hidden about.

Through tangled thoughts and embered dreams,
Life flows on in silent streams.
In every pause, a chance to feel,
Words unspoken, so surreal.

Yet in the quiet, hope still gleams,
For love can bloom in whispered dreams.
In every space where silence sways,
Words unspoken pave the ways.

A Memory Dressed in Black

In shadows deep, where whispers fade,
Echos linger of choices made.
A haunting figure, cloaked in night,
Calls to me with a ghostly light.

The past, a tapestry of tears,
Frayed and worn through fleeting years.
Each thread a story, vibrant, stark,
Yet all remain in shades of dark.

Time's cruel hand, it pulls away,
Tomorrow's dawn, a price to pay.
Yet in that silence, hope may bloom,
A flicker soft amid the gloom.

With every sigh, a tale unfolds,
Of love and loss, of dreams retold.
A memory dressed in black, it stays,
In corners where my heart still sways.

But through the veil of blackened night,
A silver star begins its flight.
Reminding me, as shadows wane,
That beauty lingers, after pain.

The Song of Regret

A melody that haunts my mind,
In every note, a truth I find.
The original tune fades away,
Replaced by words I did not say.

Each stanza holds a silent plea,
For moments lost, for you and me.
Regrets arouse with every chord,
In harmony, my heart is bored.

The verses twist, the rhythm slows,
A broken heart that never knows.
Such sweet despair, a bitter taste,
The song lingers, the time we waste.

Yet somewhere in this haunting sound,
A flicker of redemption's found.
I may have strayed beyond the light,
But still, I long for what was right.

So let the music play once more,
Though tinged with shades of what's before.
I'll mend the notes, I'll sing anew,
For in this song, I'm lost in you.

Ephemeral Promises

Upon the dawn, we made a vow,
With hopes that sparkled like the dew.
Yet life unfurled its tangled thread,
And dreams slipped softly through the red.

Each whisper shared, a fleeting breeze,
Like autumn leaves that dance with ease.
Promises in twilight wane,
Bright glimmers lost to falling rain.

In fragile moments, bonds were cast,
Yet time, relentless, moves so fast.
Amid the laughter, shadows creep,
In silence, all our secrets seep.

But still, I hold those moments dear,
Though shadows loom and disappear.
Ephemeral though they may seem,
They linger bright, like faded dreams.

So here's to love that sparks, then fades,
To fleeting joys the heart parades.
For in each promise, brief yet true,
Our souls entwine, in shades of blue.

Shattered Rose Petals

A garden once, in bloom so bright,
Now rests in shards, a lost delight.
The petals fall, like whispers low,
Of love once felt, now laid to foe.

In morning light, the remnants lay,
A fragrant past that slipped away.
Each fragment soft, a tale untold,
Of tender hearts that lost their hold.

Yet through the cracks, new life may spring,
A daring hope, a fragile thing.
For even in the harshest lands,
Resilience blooms, despite life's hands.

So gather up the broken pieces,
In every loss, a strength increases.
Shattered rose petals, beauty flawed,
In nature's art, we find our God.

Though love may fade, it leaves a trace,
In every heart, a sacred space.
For memories linger, not in vain,
While shattered rose petals dance in rain.

The Farewell Tune

As dusk descends with soft embrace,
A melody of memories trace.
Each note a whisper of goodbye,
In twilight's arms, we start to sigh.

The chords we played now linger still,
With every heartbeat, every thrill.
The laughter shared, the tearful nights,
Now echo softly in the heights.

The time is here, the song must end,
Yet in our hearts, the love won't bend.
We carry forth this final sound,
In every step, it will be found.

Though shadows fall and silence reigns,
The farewell tune forever gains.
In every parting, every ache,
A sacred bond is what we make.

So let the music play once more,
In memories, we still explore.
Through every note, in every line,
The farewell tune will always shine.

Heartstrings Untuned

In quiet halls, the echoes fade,
Where laughter built, now memories made.
A symphony of hearts once tight,
Now untuned, lost in the night.

Each strum of fate, a bitter sound,
In silence, we can hear it pound.
A rhythm tossed, a dance undone,
With every heartbeat, comes the sun.

The strings that held our hopes in place,
Now tremble, seek a new embrace.
Yet in this loss, we find a way,
To weave new chords for another day.

The pages turned, the music sways,
In fractured notes, love still conveys.
Though heartstrings pull and sometimes fray,
Together, we'll find a brighter way.

Navigating the Echoes

Through corridors of time we glide,
Where voices linger, where thoughts collide.
Each echo whispers tales of old,
In every shadow, stories told.

We wander paths of joy and pain,
Navigating through the rain.
A compass forged from memory,
Guides us through the reverie.

With every step, the echoes sigh,
Reminding us of days gone by.
Past laughter dances on the breeze,
In every rustle of the leaves.

The journey weaves a tapestry,
Of love, of loss, of history.
In echoes deep and silence strong,
We find the place where we belong.

So let us forge ahead with grace,
In echoes, we will find our place.
Through every sound, our hearts will roam,
Navigating to our true home.

The Last Candle Burns

In flickering light, the shadows play,
As night descends, we drift away.
The last candle burns, its flame so bright,
Illuminates the depths of night.

Warmth in the glow, a soft embrace,
Where time stands still in gentle space.
Each flicker tells a story near,
A whisper of love, a song we hear.

Though darkness creeps, the light remains,
A testament to joy and pains.
In every heartbeat, every glow,
The last candle's warmth will surely flow.

With every breath, we share this weight,
The flame of memories, love's fate.
As moments pass, we find our way,
In glowing light, we choose to stay.

So let the candle's warmth inspire,
A light within that will not tire.
Through shadows deep, our spirits learn,
In every heart, the last candle burns.

Reflections in Water

Beneath the surface, shadows play,
Whispers twirl in the gentle sway.
Dreams flicker, then start to blend,
In the calm, all stories mend.

Moonlight dances on each wave,
Secrets told, the quiet brave.
Every ripple, a tale to share,
Life's journey keeps us unaware.

Colors shimmer, bright and deep,
Lost in thoughts that softly creep.
Nature's mirror, clear and bright,
Reflects our hearts in pale moonlight.

In the depths, we search for peace,
From the chaos, we find release.
Rippling truths begin to show,
In the stillness, we learn to grow.

With every glance, a chance to see,
The beauty in simplicity.
In tranquil waters, lives entwine,
Reflections whisper, all is fine.

Unwritten Endings

The story pauses, ink stands still,
A blank page waits with quiet thrill.
Every choice, a path unseen,
In the silence, hopes convene.

Moments linger, lost in time,
Dreams unspoken, rhythm and rhyme.
A heart that beats with fervent grace,
Yearns for words to find their place.

Future chapters, shadows lurk,
In the silence, we find the work.
Life's a draft, a tale to weave,
In the endings, we believe.

Unfinished thoughts, a painter's dream,
On cloths of white, we dare to scheme.
In the gaps, our voices soar,
Writing futures, forevermore.

Each breath a word, each step a line,
In unwritten tomes, we shine.
Embrace the unknown, chase the light,
In every ending, a new delight.

The Road Less Traveled

Two paths diverge in morning mist,
One calls softly, one persists.
Curious hearts walk on alone,
Tracing dreams, where seeds are sown.

Through tangled woods, the unknown calls,
In the distance, a soft wind thralls.
Each footstep echoes, brave and bold,
In whispered tales, adventures unfold.

The path is rough, the journey long,
Yet in the struggle, we find our song.
Turning corners, we face the fear,
Each twist and turn brings wisdom near.

Often lost but never done,
With every stumble, new paths run.
Journeys shape who we become,
On roads less traveled, hearts grow numb.

With open eyes, we venture forth,
In every choice, we find our worth.
The road unknown, a chance to thrive,
A testament to being alive.

Mosaic of Melancholy

In shadows cast by fading light,
Fragments dance, both dark and bright.
Heartfelt pieces scatter wide,
A tapestry where sorrows bide.

Colors blend, a sorrowed hue,
In every loss, a love that's true.
Moments captured, briefly shown,
In aching hearts, we find our own.

Jigsaw puzzles yet undone,
Memories linger, one by one.
In silent echoes, laughter fades,
As twilight softly serenades.

Yet in the cracks, hope glimmers bright,
A mosaic formed in fading light.
Beauty rises from the tears,
Resilience born from hidden fears.

Wrap me close in this embrace,
In every fragment, find my place.
A masterpiece with tales to tell,
In melancholy, we all dwell.

Remnants of a Dream

In twilight's glow, whispers fade,
Fragments of hope, memories laid.
Stars twinkle softly, shadows sigh,
Echoes of laughter that drift and die.

Worn pages hold tales of old,
Silent secrets, hopes untold.
Between the lines, glimmers of grace,
Fleeting moments we can trace.

The night's embrace, a gentle shroud,
Fading echoes lost in the crowd.
What once was bright, now whispers mere,
Remnants remain, though dreams disappear.

Each broken promise, a haunting sound,
In the maze of dreams, lost I'm found.
In this quiet space, I still believe,
In remnants of dreams, I shall weave.

Time's Relentless Passage

As sands slip through, we stand in awe,
Moments fleeting, governed by law.
A clock ticks onward, hearts align,
With memories held in the hands of time.

Days blend into a timeless stream,
Lost in the fabric of every dream.
Echoes of laughter, shadows play,
The past remains, though we've drifted away.

Seasons turn like pages worn,
In every sunset, a new dawn is born.
Time's gentle hand strokes the face,
Of lives intertwined in a tender grace.

Moments captured in whispered sighs,
In the cadence of time, a love that never dies.
Each fleeting second, a gift we keep,
In time's relentless passage, memories deep.

The Color of Solitude

In quiet hues, the heart finds peace,
A canvas stretched, where worries cease.
Whispers of teal, gentle and soft,
In solitude's grip, we rise aloft.

The world outside fades to gray,
As colors bloom in a vibrant display.
A splash of cerulean, the warmth of gold,
In solitude's silence, stories unfold.

A palette of heartbeats, tranquil and rare,
Each brushstroke speaks, though none are there.
Crimson and amber, shadows embrace,
In solitude's arms, we find our place.

With every hue, the soul expresses,
Through quiet moments, emotion confesses.
In the dance of colors, solace we find,
In the color of solitude, hearts entwined.

Paper Cranes in the Rain

Folding hope in the hands of dreams,
Paper cranes float on silver streams.
A dance of wishes in the storm,
Each crease tells tales against the norm.

Beneath gray skies, they twist and glide,
Fragile whispers, where hopes reside.
With every drop, new dreams take flight,
In the heart of rain, their spirits ignite.

Cascading waters, a gentle embrace,
Cradling dreams in a soft place.
With every flutter, they seek the sky,
Paper cranes in the rain, soaring high.

Through puddles deep, reflections bloom,
In the art of flight, there's room to loom.
They chase the clouds, unbound, untamed,
In paper's fragility, hope is named.

Lighthouses Dimmed

In the fog, a beacon fades,
Waves crash on the tethered shore.
Memories of light cascade,
Whispers of the days before.

Time erodes the concrete strong,
Guiding lights dulled by the night.
Voices lost in the siren's song,
Fading echoes, dimmed from sight.

Once they stood, steadfast and bright,
Now they falter, shadows blend.
Hopes flicker in the depth of night,
Lonely keepers, dreams descend.

What remains in the twilight glow?
Ghostly tales of sailors brave.
The lighthouse stands, but hard to know,
Only darkness, only waves.

In their place, a memory clings,
Silent watch over the vast sea.
Time forgets what love still sings,
For lighthouses dimmed can't be free.

Etched in Silence

Words unspoken, linger long,
Carved in shadows of the past.
Moments lost, but still they're strong,
Memories in silence cast.

The air is thick with what could be,
Glimmers of a thought unshared.
In the stillness, we both see,
Love's foundation, bold yet scared.

Time stretches thin like fragile lace,
Where laughter once would fill the room.
A tender touch replaces grace,
In the silence, there's a gloom.

Yet in this hush, a spark remains,
Chasing echoes that resonate.
In the quiet, silence reigns,
Telling tales, we still await.

Etched in silence, hearts collide,
In the void, a gentle fight.
For every word that we have tried,
In unison, we find our light.

Maps of What Was

Faded trails upon the ground,
Paths once walked, now overgrown.
In each turn, lost tales abound,
Memories of a love well known.

Cartography of time gone by,
Every line tells of a place.
We chased dreams beneath the sky,
Now they're shadows that we face.

With paper crumpled, ink stains speak,
Whispers of the lives we've led.
Every marker holds a peak,
Of laughter shared and words unsaid.

But maps can fade, and hearts can stray,
Yet we chart the paths anew.
In the distance, we find our way,
Navigating skies of blue.

In every heartbeat, hope persists,
Tracing where our journeys twine.
For in the maps of what exists,
We find love's endless design.

Beneath the Stars We No Longer Share

Once we danced 'neath cosmic light,
Promises made in midnight's glow.
Now the stars escape our sight,
Fading dreams, the winds now blow.

Whispers carried on the breeze,
Starlight shines for hearts once bold.
Through the void, memories tease,
In the silence, stories told.

We reach for galaxies unseen,
But the space feels unfamiliar.
Having wandered, we're caught in between,
Remnants of the past, a killer.

Yet hope twinkles in darkened skies,
With every flicker, shadows retreat.
For even when the distance lies,
Love's reflection can't be beat.

Beneath the stars, our dreams have soared,
Though pathways part and time does wane.
Connections forged, forever stored,
In the universe, still remain.

Navigating the Void

In shadows deep, I wander slow,
The stars above seem faintly glow.
Each step I take, the silence grows,
In the void, my spirit flows.

Echoes call from distant dreams,
I search for light, or so it seems.
Through endless night and time's cruel jest,
I seek a place that feels like rest.

A compass made of whispered sighs,
Map my heart, as darkness flies.
In the quiet, I find my voice,
Amidst the void, I've made my choice.

With every breath, I feel the change,
Familiar paths begin to range.
The void transforms beneath my feet,
In the darkness, I'm complete.

Though lost I seem, I understand,
The void is vast, yet holds my hand.
Through cosmic tides, I weave my fate,
In navigating, I create.

The Softest Goodnight

The moonlight spills, a gentle stream,
Whispering secrets, as soft as a dream.
Crickets sing their lullaby,
While stars wink down from the velvet sky.

A blanket woven of twilight's grace,
Wraps the world in its warm embrace.
Each breath I take, the silence sighs,
In this moment, the heart flies.

The night unfurls like petals wide,
Cradled in peace, I softly bide.
With every blink, my spirit soars,
In dreams, I tread on distant shores.

A fleeting thought, a tender sigh,
As sleep returns, I close my eyes.
In the softest goodnight's embrace,
I find my solace, my sacred space.

Let the moon weave silver threads,
Embrace the night as daylight sheds.
Rest comes softly, like a sigh,
The world asleep, as I float by.

Dreams Like Paper Cranes

In quiet corners of the mind,
Fragments of hope are seldom blind.
Folding wishes, one by one,
In the silence, dreams have spun.

With every crease, a story's told,
In delicate paper, visions bold.
Each crane released into the night,
Carries whispers of pure delight.

The winds of fate take them far,
Across the cosmos, past each star.
A dance of magic in the air,
Dreams take flight without a care.

In paper wings, there lies a grace,
Reflections of our heart's true place.
They soar above, they glide and glide,
Chasing light on the evening tide.

So let us fold our hopes in kind,
And scatter dreams, as love aligned.
For in our hands, they come alive,
Like paper cranes, we learn to thrive.

Weaving Solitude

In the quiet, I find my thread,
Weaving stories, where few have tread.
Each stitch a moment, rich and bold,
In solitude, my heart unfolds.

A tapestry of soft and bright,
Colors mingling in the fading light.
The loom of life, with gentle hands,
Creates a dance, where silence stands.

I gather whispers from the breeze,
Embroider dreams with utmost ease.
Patterns form, both strange and clear,
In this solitude, I hold dear.

With every knot, I gain a voice,
A symphony of thought and choice.
In quiet moments, life takes shape,
Weaving patterns that will escape.

So let the world go spinning 'round,
In this cocoon, my peace I've found.
With threads of solitude and grace,
I weave my heart, my sacred space.

Wings of Parting

In the dawn's soft light we rise,
With dreams that kissed the morning skies.
Yet time unfurls its silent thread,
And whispers love, though hearts may dread.

A gentle breeze, a fleeting glance,
In moments lost, we find our chance.
Though paths may split, our souls entwine,
In shadowed ways, your heart is mine.

Through tears that fall like summer rain,
We linger on in joy and pain.
With every step, we learn to fly,
On wings of parting, we say goodbye.

A final note, soft echoes start,
Symphonies woven in the heart.
Though silence fills the vacant space,
Love still survives, a warm embrace.

So as we part, remember this,
In every ending, there's a kiss.
A promise held beyond the time,
In memories sweet, we'll always climb.

Dreams in the Ashes

In the quiet night, the embers glow,
Whispers of dreams from long ago.
Ashes dance in the moonlight's grace,
Echoes of hope in a forgotten place.

Each flicker tells of stories lost,
Of loves once held, but at what cost?
In the silence, their shadows roam,
Finding solace, they call it home.

From the flames, new visions rise,
With open hearts and brightened skies.
The past may fade, but flames ignite,
Rebirth of dreams in the darkest night.

Through trials faced, we come alive,
In ashes cold, our spirits thrive.
Seeds of hope in the heart replant,
From the void, new visions chant.

So let the flames consume the pain,
With every ending, something gained.
From ashes cold, the future beams,
Awake, we rise, and reclaim dreams.

The Art of Letting Go

In gardens green, where wildflowers grow,
We learn the art of letting go.
With every petal, we release our fears,
And brush away the bitter tears.

A gentle breeze, a sigh, a plea,
In nature's hands, we find the key.
With every breath, we set things free,
Embracing change, the heart's decree.

Old shadows fade as light breaks through,
In moments lost, we start anew.
Each memory, a thread we weave,
In fabric strong, we still believe.

Though paths may wind and storms may rage,
We dance through life, we turn the page.
The chords of love, forever play,
As we let go, we find our way.

So take my hand, let's face the dawn,
In letting go, our spirits bond.
With open hearts and dreams aflame,
We find our way, we rise again.

Sunsets of the Soul

As daylight fades, the horizon glows,
Painting skies with crimson flows.
Each sunset whispers secrets deep,
In silent moments, the heart will leap.

With colors bright, our stories blend,
In twilight's grasp, we round the bend.
The soft embrace of evening air,
Awakens dreams beyond compare.

In this hush, our hearts unfold,
In twilight's warmth, we are consoled.
With golden rays, we cherish time,
As shadows stretch, our souls align.

In every hue, a memory calls,
The laughter echoes, the silence falls.
We weave our tales beneath the stars,
In sunsets bright, we heal our scars.

So let the dusk unveil the night,
In each farewell, there's hope in sight.
For in the dark, we find the goal,
As journeys start with sunsets of the soul.

The Fadeaway Dance

In twilight's glow, we sway so slow,
Our shadows blend, where soft winds blow.
With every step, the world unwinds,
In whispered dreams, our hearts align.

Each twirl recalls the days long past,
A fleeting glance, a hold so fast.
In memories held, we find our chance,
To linger still in this fadeaway dance.

The music fades, yet we remain,
In silent halls, we share our pain.
With every note, a tear may fall,
Yet in this dance, we face it all.

Through shadows cast, our love ignites,
In hidden places, the dark ignites.
The whispers low, the heartbeats loud,
In gentle sway, we stand unbowed.

So let the night slip into dawn,
Our dance eternal, never gone.
With every breath, forever stay,
In faith and trust, we'll find our way.

In the Wake of Sorrow

The clouds roll in, a heavy shroud,
Silence lingers, thick like a crowd.
With every heartbeat, grief takes its toll,
In every tear, we feel the whole.

Yet in the dark, a flicker glows,
A spark of hope, where kindness grows.
With gentle words, we mend the pain,
In shared burdens, love remains.

The dawn will come, the light will break,
Though shadows linger, we will wake.
In every sorrow, seeds of grace,
Will bloom anew in this weary place.

Through whispers soft, we hold the past,
In the heart's echo, memories last.
With open arms, we face the night,
In the wake of sorrow, we find the light.

So lean on me, let's walk this path,
Through all the storms, through all the wrath.
Together strong, we will endure,
In love's embrace, we find the cure.

Memories in Dust

In quiet corners, shadows cling,
Dust settles down, the memories sing.
Forgotten toys on wooden shelves,
Echoes of laughter, the child ourselves.

Photos yellowed, frames all askew,
Faces we loved, now fading too.
Yet in each fold of creased pages,
Lie tales of joy, love's endless stages.

The attic holds secrets, whispers long,
In the grainy light, where we belong.
A gentle breeze through an open door,
Brings back the moments we can't ignore.

With every dust motes that dance in air,
Comes the laughter, the quiet despair.
In memories trapped, we find our worth,
For every end leads to a new birth.

So let us gather, let us explore,
The treasures hidden behind each door.
In memories held, we find our trust,
In time's embrace, we're more than dust.

The Echo of Empty Rooms

In the stillness, whispers roam,
The echo of what was once home.
Each corner holds a story clear,
Of joy and laughter, now shed a tear.

The walls once filled with life so bright,
Now shadows linger, lost in the night.
With every creak, the past awakes,
In empty rooms, a heartache breaks.

Photographs linger on the floor,
Moments captured, but nevermore.
In quiet spaces, we find the traces,
Of love that thrived in tender embraces.

The air is thick with memories sweet,
In every silence, our hearts still meet.
Though empty rooms may seem so stark,
The echoes of love will leave a mark.

So let us cherish, though we must part,
The echoes remain within each heart.
In every corner, the past will bloom,
For love endures in empty rooms.

Echoes of a Distant Serenade

In twilight hues, the whispers play,
A song that travels far away.
Old trees hum softly in the night,
While stars blink on with gentle light.

Beneath the moon, a shadow sways,
The nightingale in soft arrays.
Each note a dream that's softly spun,
A serenade, the heart's own sun.

The river holds its breath to hear,
The echoes calling crystal clear.
With every beat, the world will sigh,
In distant lands where memories lie.

A breeze carries tales of yore,
Of love once lost, of hearts that soar.
In every chord, a story weaves,
Of hope and heartache, joy and grieves.

So listen close, the night reveals,
The serenade that timeless heals.
In every echo, find your way,
As shadows dance with light's own play.

The Color of Departing Light

The sun dips low, a fiery red,
A canvas drawn as day has fled.
With whispers sweet, the evening glows,
In shades of gold, the twilight flows.

Clouds brush softly, pink and blue,
As nature bids the day adieu.
Each moment lingers, softly spun,
In hues that change, the day's last run.

Stars awaken in the deep,
While night unveils its secrets to keep.
The air turns cool, a gentle sigh,
Beneath the vast and endless sky.

Time stands still in this embrace,
Where shadows dance with quiet grace.
With every breath, the dusk ignites,
The beauty found in fading lights.

Embrace the dusk, let worries fade,
In every hue, a promise made.
For in the night, new dreams ignite,
The color of departing light.

Fragile Echoes

In whispers soft, the memories call,
A touch so light, yet holding all.
The fragile moments float like dust,
In quiet corners, dreams we trust.

Each echo lingers, sweet and brief,
A tender stitch of joy and grief.
In every heartbeat, past resides,
A tapestry where love abides.

The laughter shared, the silent tears,
In fragile fragments, woven years.
With every glance, a story spun,
In fleeting glances, two become one.

The colors fade, yet still they shine,
In shadows drawn, a subtle line.
As twilight's breath whispers our way,
The echoes linger, night turns to day.

Hold fast to what the heart believes,
In fragile echoes, life achieves.
For though they fade like morning dew,
The echoes stay, forever true.

A Symphony of Solitude

In silence deep, the heart will speak,
A symphony where dreams may seek.
The notes of longing gently rise,
In solitude, the spirit flies.

Each breath a chord, each thought a song,
In whispered tones where I belong.
The quiet hours, they hold a grace,
In stillness found, I find my place.

The world outside, a distant hum,
In solitude, I hear the drum.
Each heartbeat, like a gentle rain,
A melody that soothes the pain.

Through twilight's veil, I softly tread,
Where shadows linger, and dreams are fed.
In every pause, the thoughts will dance,
A symphony of sweet romance.

So let me dwell in quiet glow,
Where solitude's sweet waters flow.
In every note, a truth imbued,
A symphony, my heart renewed.

Abandoned Promises

Whispers of dreams left behind,
Shadows dance in the twilight.
Faded echoes of what could be,
Time wends on, a silent blight.

Words once sweet, now bitter tears,
Lost in the wind, drifting away.
Hearts once joined, now broken seams,
Hope fades with the end of day.

Empty echoes fill the night,
Unraveled tales of fleeting trust.
Promises fall like autumn leaves,
Lost in the dust, turned to rust.

Eyes watching the fading light,
Longing for what was once near.
Paths diverged, souls left alone,
In silence, I wipe a tear.

But in the dark, a spark remains,
Memories linger, soft and bright.
Though abandoned, that flicker stays,
Guiding me through lost night.

The Lament of Lost Moments

Ticking clocks mark time's cruel race,
Each second slips like grains of sand.
Fleeting laughter haunts the air,
Ghosts of joy, mere shadows stand.

Days that shimmer, now tucked away,
Faded smiles whisper in vain.
Promises made during bright days,
Dissolve like mist in the rain.

I reach for you in empty space,
Longing lingers, bittersweet.
Moments danced slip through my hands,
An endless ache, incomplete.

Old photographs, a haunting glow,
Stale memories trapped in frames.
Who we were and what we lost,
Echoes still call out our names.

Yet here I stand, with open heart,
Embracing shadows of the past.
In loss, I find a quiet strength,
In each lament, love's shadows cast.

Solitary Starlight

Underneath a blanket vast,
Stars ignite the night's embrace.
Whispers of dreams shaped in light,
Guided by time's gentle grace.

Alone I wander, skyward gaze,
Each twinkle a story, untold.
Chasing visions through the haze,
In solitude, the night unfolds.

Celestial rhythms softly call,
Tracing paths that bend and sway.
In the cosmos, I am one,
Yet find my peace in disarray.

The universe, a friend and foe,
In silence, I find my voice.
Each star a wish from long ago,
In solitude, the heart seeks choice.

For in this vastness, hope shines bright,
Illuminating every tear.
Solitary starlight guides,
Through darkened paths, no more fear.

Buried Hopes

In the garden of what once bloomed,
Hopes are buried deep in earth.
Seeds of longing, dreams entombed,
Waiting for a second birth.

Tendrils stretch toward the sun,
Pushing through the weight of doubt.
Though hidden from the light of day,
Life's promise whispers, "Do not shout."

Time will nurture, rain will fall,
Soft caress of fate's own hand.
Sprouts emerging, breaking walls,
Reclaiming life in this land.

Each tear once shed, a drop of rain,
Watering long-forgotten dreams.
Buried hopes now rise again,
In the silence, new life gleams.

What was lost, now found anew,
Hope's resilience shines so clear.
From the ashes, blooms come through,
Buried treasures reappear.

Fragments of a Once-Whole Heart

Scattered pieces on the floor,
Memories whispering evermore.
Love that once felt strong and bright,
Now a shadow in the night.

Hopes have faded, lost to time,
Echoes of an unbroken rhyme.
We dance around the empty space,
Grief etched deep upon my face.

Each fragment tells a different tale,
Of joy once loved, now frail.
In silence, secrets start to part,
Leaving me with a broken heart.

Yet still I gather, piece by piece,
Searching for a chance of peace.
In my chest, a yearning beat,
For a love that felt complete.

I hold these shards, both sharp and sweet,
With every step, I face defeat.
But in the cracks, new light can spark,
Illuminating paths from dark.

Ghosts of Forgotten Laughter

In hollow halls, the echoes linger,
Whispers resonate like a singer.
Joy once danced upon these floors,
Now it's trapped behind closed doors.

Footsteps trace the moments past,
Fleeting joy that did not last.
Faces fade, but smiles remain,
The shadows still hold their refrain.

In quiet corners, joy once bloomed,
Now it's wrapped in dust and gloom.
Memories drift like autumn leaves,
Haunting vibes that never leave.

Time moves on, yet still they cling,
To laughter's soft and fleeting ring.
Ghostly forms of days gone by,
In dreams, I hear their gentle sigh.

I chase these echoes, warm and bright,
Through the veil of fading light.
For in the laughter that we shared,
Is a love that always cared.

The Space Between Us

An empty void, a silent plea,
Yearning hearts weave destiny.
Between the stars, the breathless night,
Holds whispers of a distant light.

Two souls adrift in tangled fate,
With unspoken words we contemplate.
Each heartbeat echoes like a drum,
Mapping paths where love can come.

In every glance, a spark ignites,
Beneath the surface, hidden sights.
Yet still the distance holds us tight,
In shadows, yearning for the light.

We reach across with trembling hands,
Building bridges, soft as sands.
For in the gap, the dreams align,
With every breath, our souls entwine.

Though miles may stretch and time may bend,
In thought, we find a way to mend.
A promise hidden in the night,
To close the space and make it right.

Ashes of Yesterday's Dreams

Once they soared, now they fall,
Whispers of a broken call.
Embers flicker in the dust,
Dreams once strong, now fade to rust.

In quiet corners, echoes sigh,
Memories linger, asking why.
Hopes that danced on fleeting wings,
Reduced to naught, such fragile things.

The canvas grey, the colors blend,
Stories whispered, hearts defend.
Yet through the ashes, light may gleam,
A chance reborn in faded dream.

From remnants, new paths can arise,
Reflections of once-brilliant skies.
To forge anew from dust once known,
In the ashes, seeds are sown.

So here I stand, with heart aflame,
Amidst the ruins, I reclaim.
For every dream that fades away,
Holds the promise of a new day.

Unwritten Letters

In shadows of the night, I write,
With words that never see the light.
A paper heart, a lover's plea,
Enclosed in silence, just for me.

Each syllable a whispered thought,
In pages worn, my dreams are caught.
They dance upon the empty page,
A timeless tale that won't age.

With ink that flows like secrets told,
A thousand stories left unrolled.
In dreams, I send them far and wide,
While holding back the tears I hide.

Will you unseal these hidden lines?
Or leave them lost in twilight shrines?
The longing lingers in the air,
Unwritten letters, love laid bare.

A flutter in the heart, a sigh,
In mute confession, I let fly.
Each letter penned, yet never sent,
A language of the soul, unbent.

A Dance with Shadows

In twilight's grasp, we softly sway,
The shadows lead, we find our way.
With every turn, the world does shift,
A waltz of dreams, a ghostly gift.

With every step, we break apart,
Yet shadows cling, they share the heart.
A flicker here, a shimmer there,
The dance ignites the evening air.

The whispering winds, our only sound,
In darkened corners, love is found.
With fleeting moments, we embrace,
In shadow's arms, we find our place.

As morning breaks, the shadows fade,
The fleeting dance, a sweet charade.
Yet in its wake, a silence stays,
A memory wrapped in twilight's haze.

The dance may halt, but not the tune,
It hums beneath the watchful moon.
In stillness now, we hold the grace,
Of shadows danced, our hearts' embrace.

Moments Caught in Time

In fleeting seconds, life unfolds,
Each heart a story, yet untold.
We chase the sunlight, run from night,
And find our truths in fleeting light.

A laughter shared, a tear that falls,
In every echo, love enthralls.
The whispers of a hidden past,
In moments caught, our shadows cast.

A glance exchanged, a hand held tight,
These sacred times ignite the night.
They twirl like leaves upon the breeze,
In every heartbeat, memories freeze.

The clock ticks on, yet still we pause,
And revel in the world's applause.
Each memory weaved with gold,
A tapestry of life behold.

For every moment, bittersweet,
Collect the gems beneath our feet.
In all these fragments, love we find,
A dance of souls forever twined.

The Fissures of Connection

In shadows deep, our spirits thread,
Through fissures wide where silence spread.
A crack appears, a fragile touch,
Where hearts collide, we yearn for much.

In whispered dreams, we start to weave,
A tapestry of hope to believe.
With every word, the gaps we mend,
Resilient souls that transcend.

Yet still the void can pull us back,
The heavy weight, a shadowed track.
With every laugh, a tear we shed,
In this dance of life, love is fed.

We search for bridges, hearts laid bare,
Through cracking ice, we find our care.
Though fissures grow, we stand as one,
United still beneath the sun.

So here we'll stand, defy the night,
In fractures bright, we find our light.
For love can heal the deepest scars,
In every fissure, hope is ours.

Frayed Threads

In the loom of time, we weave,
Silken dreams that softly fray.
Every thread a tale we leave,
Fading colors, dusk to day.

Moments slip like grains of sand,
Ties that bind begin to tear.
Holding close a trembling hand,
Wishing still for what we share.

Memories, a patchwork quilt,
Holding warmth in every seam.
Life is marked by love we built,
Even when it breaks the dream.

With each stitch, a hope unspun,
Yet we find strength in the fray.
Though the fabric's come undone,
Love remains, it finds a way.

Every thread a part of us,
Woven in both joy and pain.
In this tapestry of trust,
We'll endure, and live again.

Seasons of Goodbye

Leaves are falling, whispers low,
Time to part, the sun must set.
Every heartbeat learns to know,
Love remains though hearts forget.

Winter comes with icy breath,
Frosted windows, shadows cast.
In the silence, echoes death,
Memories of moments past.

Spring will bloom with hope anew,
Yet the echoes linger on.
As the petals drink the dew,
New beginnings greet the dawn.

Summer's warmth brings laughter bright,
But the autumn calls our name.
In the cycle, day and night,
All that's lost still feels the same.

Seasons turn, and so must we,
In the warmth, in the cold lie.
Though it's hard, we'll learn to see,
Love's a path, not just goodbye.

The Broken Mirror

Cracks reflect the light of day,
Fractured pieces, shards of truth.
Each reflection leads astray,
Memories of long-lost youth.

In the glass, we see our fears,
Images of what once was.
Tears have stained our silent years,
Echoes haunting with their cause.

Finding beauty in the flaws,
Every break a story made.
Though we've stumbled, we have laws,
Strength is found in light and shade.

Hold the glass, embrace the pain,
Learn from all the broken dreams.
In our hearts, we'll find the gain,
Life is more than just it seems.

From the shards, we'll shape a whole,
Woven in this dance of fate.
In the mirror, find your soul,
Reflections of love can wait.

Shadows of Yesterday

In the dusk, shadows take flight,
Whisper secrets to the night.
Fading echoes, stories told,
Lingering warmth, a heart so bold.

Every moment whispers low,
Footsteps echo, soft and slow.
In the twilight, dreams reside,
Where the past and present bide.

Lost in time, we find our way,
Memories of yesterday.
In the silence, hear the call,
Longing just to give our all.

Yet the dawn will break at last,
Shadows fleeting, holding fast.
As the sun begins to rise,
Hope will dance, dispelling lies.

In the light, we stand anew,
Shadows fade, the world feels true.
From the past, we find our song,
In each note, we all belong.

The Final Embrace

In twilight's hush, we meet again,
Our shadows dance, a soft refrain.
The moonlit paths lead us in grace,
In every sigh, the final embrace.

A whisper lingers on the breeze,
Two hearts entwined, as time does freeze.
Each beat a promise, tender and true,
In the silence, I find you too.

The stars ignite our secret song,
In this moment, we both belong.
The world fades out, we're lost in night,
Hold me close, everything feels right.

With every breath, the past released,
In love's soft arms, we find our peace.
Together woven, soft and warm,
In the final embrace, we transform.

As dawn approaches, light will break,
Yet in this heartbeat, nothing fakes.
Forever etched in memory's space,
We'll cherish still, the final embrace.

Fragments of a Heartbeat

In the quiet, whispers blend,
Fragments of dreams that never end.
A heartbeat echoes, soft and clear,
In every sound, I hold you near.

The rhythm dances beneath the stars,
Carving moments from the scars.
Each pulse a story yet untold,
In fragments, our love unfolds.

Time stands still, a gentle sigh,
With every glance, we learn to fly.
Amidst the chaos, we find our way,
In fragments of what dreams convey.

A fading sunset paints the sky,
In every color, you and I.
Together woven, like threads of light,
In fragments, we conquer the night.

The heart beats strong, with passion's fire,
In every moment, we reach higher.
As fragments merge, we find our art,
In every heartbeat, a brand new start.

Threads of Caprice

In moonlight's glow, our paths entwine,
Threads of caprice, a dance divine.
We weave our tales with laughter bright,
In every moment, pure delight.

Like winds that whisper through the leaves,
In playful murmurs, the heart believes.
Each twist and turn, a fresh surprise,
In threads of caprice, love never dies.

We paint the skies with dreams anew,
In every shade, I see you too.
A canvas vast, where hopes reside,
In threads we hold, forever tied.

Life's tapestry, a vibrant hue,
Interwoven stories, me and you.
Though storms may toss and winds may sear,
In threads of caprice, love stays near.

Through winding roads, our journeys flow,
A dance of chance, where we both grow.
In every stitch, passion's embrace,
Together we laugh at threads of caprice.

Silence Speaks

In the stillness, silence reigns,
A language spoken, yet unchained.
Between the words, a world unfolds,
In silence speaks what the heart holds.

The echoes linger, soft and low,
In quiet corners, feelings glow.
No need for sound, as we find peace,
In silence speaks, our love's release.

A gaze exchanged, a tender thread,
In every moment, all that's said.
The space between us, softly swells,
In silence speaks, our truth compels.

When storms may rage, and voices clash,
In the calm, our fears will dash.
Together wrapped, in evening's cloak,
In silence speaks, the words unspoke.

As dawn breaks forth, the light will beam,
Yet in this stillness, we still dream.
For in the hush, we find our way,
In silence speaks, we'll always stay.

The Final Note

In shadows deep, the silence reigns,
A melody lost, where sorrow pains.
Fingers trembling, I pen the last,
A haunting refrain from the past.

Echoes linger, the room is bare,
Each note a tear, a whispered prayer.
The clock ticks down, time slips away,
In the final note, my heart will stay.

Glimmers of hope in the fading light,
Yet darkness falls, swallowing bright.
With every chord, I feel the ache,
A lasting song that love did make.

Goodbye to dreams that softly called,
In this final note, I find I'm small.
A world once full, now fades from sight,
Carried away on wings of night.

So here I sit, pen in my hand,
Writing my fate in a desolate land.
The final note, a solemn vow,
In a quiet end, I whisper now.

Ghost Town of the Heart

Once vibrant streets now echo pain,
An empty dance, a forgotten strain.
Laughter lost in the dusty air,
Memories linger, but none to share.

Windows shattered, doors ajar,
Whispers of dreams left where they are.
The twilight fades, the shadows grow,
Haunting the spaces we used to know.

Footsteps falter on broken stone,
Each step taken feels so alone.
A heart once full now wears a crown,
Of hollowed hopes in this ghost town.

No songs of love to light the way,
Just echoes of joy from a brighter day.
In this silence, the truth is stark,
The ghost town of a faded heart.

Yet in the dusk, where shadows play,
I seek a spark to guide the way.
For even in ruins, life can start,
A flicker of hope in the ghost town heart.

Empty Vows

Whispers sweet in the morning light,
Promises made under starlit night.
Words like petals drift in the air,
But time has shown how little they care.

Once held tightly, now they slip free,
Empty echoes of what used to be.
Vows once cherished, now turn to dust,
Trust fractured thin, just shadows of us.

The warmth of love has turned to chill,
Each empty vow cold against the will.
Forgotten dreams lie scattered around,
In silent spaces where love once found.

A fleeting glance, a distant sigh,
In the heart's quiet, where love must die.
We trace the lines where we swore to stay,
Yet each promise fades, washed away.

But in the rubble, seeds may grow,
In the soil of loss, new blooms can show.
For even empty vows have their grace,
A chance for healing, a different space.

The Twilight Hour

When day surrenders to night's embrace,
The twilight hour finds its place.
Colors bleed in the fading sky,
As dreams awaken, and shadows lie.

A gentle hush blankets the land,
Where time slows down, and hearts expand.
In this moment, all fears dissolve,
Whispers of dusk invite us to evolve.

Stars emerge with a timid glow,
As secrets of night begin to flow.
The moon casts silver on quiet streams,
While the world holds tight to lingering dreams.

A dance of light in a velvet sea,
The twilight hour sets weary hearts free.
Each heartbeat synchronized with the night,
A harmony found in soft twilight.

Breathe in deep as the shadows play,
In the twilight hour, worries decay.
Here in this space, we find our power,
And lose ourselves in the twilight hour.